*f*P

ALSO BY GARY ZUKAV

The Dancing Wu Li Masters:
An Overview of the New Physics

The Seat of the Soul

Thoughts from The Seat of the Soul:
Meditations for Souls in Process

Soul Stories

WITH LINDA FRANCIS

The Heart of the Soul:
Emotional Awareness

Thoughts from The Heart of the Soul:
Meditations for Emotional Awareness

SELF-EMPOWERMENT
JOURNAL

A Companion to

THE
MIND
OF THE
SOUL
Responsible Choice

Gary Zukav
and
Linda Francis

FREE PRESS
New York   London   Toronto   Sydney   Singapore

*f*P

FREE PRESS
A Division of Simon & Schuster, Inc.
1230 Avenue of the Americas
New York, NY 10020

First Free Press trade paperback edition 2003

FREE PRESS and colophon are
trademarks of Simon & Schuster, Inc.

For information about special discounts for bulk purchases,
please contact Simon & Schuster Special Sales at
1-800-456-6798 or business@simonandschuster.com

Designed by Jamie Putorti
Illustrations by Melanie Parks

Manufactured in the United States of America

1   3   5   7   9   10   8   6   4   2

Library of Congress Cataloging-in-Publication Data is available.

ISBN 0-7432-5746-4

This book is dedicated to my parents,
Teresa Compton and the late Hugh Compton,
with love and appreciation.
—Linda Francis

Contents

PART 5: *Responsible Choice*

Welcome

Welcome to this special Self-Empowerment Journal. It is designed to accompany our book *The Mind of the Soul: Responsible Choice.*

Our intention for creating this Journal is very specific: We want to help you create authentic power—the alignment of your personality with your soul. Responsible choice is one of the essential skills you will need to create authentic power. As you develop the ability to choose responsibly, you will simultaneously become more powerful.

In this Journal we will do what we can to:

- Show you the difference between authentic power and external power, and the role of responsible choice in creating authentic power.
- Help you understand responsible choice intellectually, experientially, and, especially, emotionally.
- Provide exercises, practices, and opportunities to create authentic power both while you are using this Journal and long after you complete it.

We do not ask you to accept what we write as true, but instead to notice what resonates with you and, when something does, experiment with it. If you like what your experiment produces, continue to experiment. If we present something with which you do not resonate, let it go. Don't try to wear a shoe that pinches. *The Mind of the Soul: Responsible Choice* and this Self-Empowerment Journal present a window through which we have come to see the world. This window has been helpful to us and we hope it will be helpful to you, too.

Love,
Gary Zukav and Linda Francis

PART 1

Choice

On a Personal Note
—*Gary*

I did not realize how important my choices are until I made the effort to look at what they had created. Even then, it took several more years for me to make the connection between what I choose and what I experience.

For example, when I graduated from Harvard I was angry, insecure, and violent. It seemed natural for me to enlist in the infantry and volunteer for the Green Berets. I was not drafted. I volunteered for more and more specialized training, bringing myself into contact with an increasingly homogeneous group of angry, insecure, and violent people. We did not look at ourselves that way. We admired ourselves and our jobs. That was because we shared the same consciousness, even though we had unique histories and challenges, and even though we sometimes did not like one another. Our skin colors, families, religious backgrounds, and the reasons that brought us together—such as running away from home, playing a heroic role, patriotism, and so forth—were different, but our energy was the same. It did not occur to me at the time that my choices about who I was and what I needed were bringing me into the company of others who were making similar choices.

Now when I look around me, I do not see any individuals like those I knew in the military. Instead I see individuals who are like me, as I am now—striving to take responsibility for their decisions, create wisely, learn from their experiences, and grow spiritually. Each of us is unique, but we share those qualities. I am no longer attracted to weapons, and I no longer have the desire to wear the uniform that once meant so much to me. I make different choices now, and so do the people who are in my life. In retrospect, I can see that the people in my life have changed, because I have changed.

1
The Power of Choice

*E*ach choice you make creates experiences for you and others. In fact, the way you perceive yourself is a choice. Choice equals creation.

How Do You Perceive Yourself?

Do you consider yourself:

Beautiful	Ugly
Smart	Stupid
Handsome	Plain
Inferior	Superior
Competent	Incompetent
Outgoing	Introverted
Brave	Cowardly
Open	Closed
Emotional	Unfeeling

Do you feel somewhere in between? Or do you feel one way sometimes, and other times another way?

Think about your characteristics. Write down the words that describe you. Take five or ten minutes to make this list.

....

....

....

....

....

....

....

....

....

....

....

....

....

....

....

....

....

....

....

Now look at each word on your list and, after each word, say to yourself, "I perceive myself as _____, and this is a choice I have made."

Focusing on what you cannot do, instead of what you can do, creates a picture of yourself that is narrow and incomplete. When you focus on your strengths, you see yourself as a competent person, because your desires and strengths are aligned.

*W*hen you make the connection between your choices and your experiences, you do not have to create the same experiences again. You can create different experiences by choosing differently. There is no limit to your creative capacity.

A Second Look

Let's look at your list again. After each word, decide if you want to continue looking at yourself that way. If not, circle that word.

Speak each circled word out loud, one at a time, and as you do, say to yourself, "I can choose to continue seeing myself as _____, or I can choose to focus on my natural aptitudes and abilities instead."

Write what you experience.

....

....

....

....

....

....

....

....

Shouting in anger,
suffering with jealousy,
and
withdrawing in fear
reflect
WHAT YOU HAVE CHOSEN
not
who you are.

As long as you feel you have behaviors you cannot change, you will be in a prison whenever anyone pushes one of your "buttons." Your options will diminish. If you are angry, jealous, or resentful enough, you will have no options at all. Until you change the part of your personality that reacts when it is frightened with anger, jealousy, or resentment, you will remain in prison.

Set Yourself Free

The next time you feel an impulse to engage in a behavior you think you cannot change, imagine that you are about to put yourself in a jail. If instead you choose to think, speak, or act differently, imagine you are walking away from a jail.

Notice when you put yourself in jail and when you set yourself free. (You may want to carry a notepad with you.)

Write your significant discoveries about yourself.

....

....

....

....

....

....

....

....

*E*ach of your painful emotions is a class in the Earth school from which you must graduate. Until you do, you will experience the destructive consequences of those emotions. How long you remain in these classes is your choice.

My Classes

List the Earth school classes you are taking, such as anger, jealousy, gratitude, vengefulness, contentment, appreciation, or fear. Decide which classes you want to complete and which classes you love to attend. Put a check mark beside the classes you want to complete.

....

....

....

....

....

....

....

....

....

....

....

Choosing is the act of creation. The most important choices you make are the choices about how you see yourself, the Universe, and your relation to the Universe. No matter what you choose, you create experiences for yourself. Your only choice is what experiences you will create.

My Most Important Choices Are

How I see myself———— How I see the Universe

My relationship with
the Universe

2
Cause and Effect

A cause and its effect are not separate. Love, reverence, hate, jealousy, contentment, gratitude, and joy are all causes in your life, and each has an effect.

*W*hen a cause occurs, so will an effect. The effect might happen quickly, or it might appear long after its cause, but it will occur.

A Week of Kindness

Go out of your way to be friendly and kind to people that you encounter during this week. Extend this kindness to people with whom you talk on the phone, email, or write. Then notice how you feel and what effects you notice in your life. Record here specific instances of the kindness you have extended, your feelings about them, and the effects you notice.

Day One

....

....

....

Day Two

....

....

....

Day Three

....

....

....

Day Four

....

....

....

Day Five

....

....

....

Day Six

....

....

....

Day Seven

....

....

....

Responsible choice is choosing the cause carefully so that you will create the effect you want.

*A*s you become multisensory, you begin to realize that not all causes are physical and not all effects are physical.

Am I Multisensory?

Make a list of the ways you can identify that you are multisensory. For example:

- I sense what decision I need to make.
- I have hunches.
- I value my insights.
- I use my intuition.
- Sometimes I know more than I can see.

*M*ultisensory humans are not satisfied with controlling more or having more. Their goal is spiritual growth, and they understand power in a new way—the alignment of the personality with the soul.

Try It Out

Remind yourself that you are multisensory. Say to yourself, "I will use my multisensory perceptions to see my challenges today as opportunities to grow spiritually." Or ask yourself, "Using my multisensory perception, how would I use my life differently today?" At the end of the day, record your observations here.

....

....

....

....

....

....

....

....

....

3

The Science of the Soul

*M*ultisensory humans are creating a new science—the science of the soul. It utilizes the dynamics that underlie physical appearances to create beneficial consequences and avoid destructive consequences. Scientists of the soul see that consciousness shapes physical reality.

Changing the consciousness that creates war, poverty, hunger, and exploitation into the consciousness that cherishes Life solves these problems permanently.

Begin to Experiment

When your consciousness is kind and loving, it creates experiences of kindness and love, and when it is violent, it creates violent experiences.

Watch yourself carefully. Notice what you do and what you say. For example:

- Do you wake up grumpy, or happy?
- Are you polite to some people and impatient with others?
- Are you doing what you love or what you would rather not do?

Begin to experiment with seeing each moment as an opportunity to choose the experience you want. Write your observations here. Be specific.

....

....

....

....

....

....

....

....

Your experiences are a mirror, and your intentions are reflected back to you by them. Your experiences will not change until your consciousness changes.

Look in the Mirror

Imagine that everything you see around you—the character of your friends, the experiences you encounter—is a mirror of your consciousness. Notice what you like and what you don't like. Do this until you feel you are getting to know your reflection.

Write here what you intend to change and what you intend to continue.

....

....

....

....

....

....

....

....

....

....

....

*W*hen you participate in a cause, you will participate in its effect. The universal law of cause and effect is called karma in the East, and the Golden Rule in the West.

Exploring the Golden Rule

Remember a time when something happened to you that you were surprised and delighted about—for example, an unexpected gift or kindness. Note it here.

....

....

....

....

....

Ask yourself, "Have I ever surprised and delighted others in a similar way?" Give an example here.

....

....

....

....

....

....

Remember when something happened and you were shocked and hurt—for example, you were betrayed, or someone became enraged at you. Note the instance here.

....

....

....

....

....

....

Ask yourself, "Have I ever shocked and hurt others in a similar way?" Write about it here.

....

....

....

....

....

....

....

The New Scientific Method:

1. *Become aware of your intentions.*
2. *Consider what each of your intentions will create.*
3. *Choose the intention that will create the consequences you desire. (This is a responsible choice.)*
4. *Observe how your experiences change.*
5. *If your experiences do not change, find the parts of your personality that hold different intentions, and change them.*
6. *Do the experiment again.*

There is no limit to the number of ways you can experiment with the Universal law of cause and effect. Every moment brings you a new opportunity.

Become a Scientist of the Soul

The next time you are not sure what consequence your action will create . . .

1. Pause.
2. Become aware of your intention.
3. Ask yourself, "What will my intention create?"
4. If you do not like your answer, try another intention.
5. Choose the intention that creates the consequence you want.
6. Notice how your experiences change, or do not change.

Reflect on your experiences and record them here. Be specific.

....

....

....

....

....

....

....

....

....

4
Attraction

Collectives pervade the human experience. Within each are more collectives, and within those are yet more. Most individuals feel more comfortable with people like themselves, unless they are trying to disown who they are.

Find Your Collectives

Make a list of the collectives you belong to. For example:

Mother	White
Student	Divorced
Male	Buddhist
Female	Businessperson
Christian	Black
American	Father
Wife	Yellow
Son	European
Asian	Daughter
Grandparent	Human

Beside each collective write a number from one to ten. Ten indicates that you identify very much with that collective. One indicates that you seldom think of yourself in terms of that collective. Notice which collectives you identify with the most.

Collective	1-10	Collective	1-10

Individuals define themselves by their collectives. The glue that holds collectives together is not language, skin color, belief, or common experience. It is fear.

The Other Side of Your Coin

Who do you separate yourself from? Take some time to think about this question. This might be a new way of looking at yourself and others, so be gentle and compassionate with yourself. Write here what you discover about yourself.

The Universal Law of Attraction

Brings people who
are loving together

Brings people who
are fearful together

And keeps them together

*W*hen you love, collectives remain, but the fortress mentality is not present, and race, sex, and history become clothes you wear, not who you are.

What is Your Identity?

Are you attached to your:

> Nationality?
> Language?
> Race?
> Personal history?
> Clothes you wear?
> Hairstyle?
> Habits?
> Religion?

Note each of your attachments below. For each, ask yourself:

- Do I feel superior to people with different attachments? If so, in what way?
- Do I feel inferior to people with different attachments? If so, how?

....

....

....

....

....

....

*Y*our experiences always validate your beliefs. Five-sensory humans say, "I will believe it when I see it." Multisensory humans know they will see it when they believe it.

Choose Your World

Choose the world you want to live in. Ask yourself questions like those below, and consider them carefully, even if you think the answers are obvious.

Do you want to live in a world of love? ....

Do you want to live in a world of fear? ....

Do you want to live in a world of exploitation? ....

Do you want to live in a world of caring people? ....

Think of other worlds you want to live in. Write down each of your choices. Then ask yourself, "What can I do to make myself the kind of person I want in my world?" Write what you discover.

....

....

....

....

....

....

....

You can attract the type of people you want in your life by becoming that type of person.

Who Do You Want in Your Life?

Pick three important characteristics you want the people you bring into your life to have. For example, "I like generous people"; "I admire people with courage"; "I want to be with people who have integrity"; etc. Make a list.

1. ....

2. ....

3. ....

Think about each of the characteristics on your list, one at a time.

- How would someone with that characteristic behave? (What would that characteristic look like?)

1. ....
....

2. ....
....

3. ....
....

- What would you feel while being around someone with that characteristic?

1. ....
....

2. ....
....

3. ....
....

- What would having someone with that characteristic in your life mean to you?

1. ....

   ....

2. ....

   ....

3. ....

   ....

Consider that to bring people with the characteristics you listed into your life, you will need to develop those characteristics yourself. For example, if you want generous people in your life, you will need to develop your own generosity. The same is true of kindness, or courage, or anything else.

Write down the things you need to change in yourself in order to attract people with the characteristics you want into your life.

....

....

....

....

....

....

*Y*ou cannot change yourself by wishing, thinking, wanting, or
desiring. You must act. When you do, you will step into a new
domain of experience, and you will find new friends there.

5

Intention

*I*ntention is the use of your will. It is the difference between having a vision and bringing it into the world.

CHOICE

is

the application

of

YOUR WILL

to

YOUR EXPERIENCE.

Y*ou create your experiences with your will, moment by moment, from your birth to your death. When consciousness is injected into the process of using your will, your experiences of life become your experiments with life.*

*T*he spiritual path is not an escape from responsibility. It is
a journey into the full depth and scope of your creative power,
and your responsibility for it.

Victim or Creator?

List the aspects of your life that you are most aware of. For example, your . . .

- Job
- Partner
- House/apartment
- Salary
- Status
- Race
- Cultural background

Ask yourself, for each aspect, which of the following statements feels more appropriate to you. Be truthful.

1. I wish this person or situation were not like this. (Victim)
2. I know this person or situation is perfect for me at this moment. (Creator)

Write a 1 or a 2 beside each aspect, to remind you of your answer.

Aspect   1 or 2

....

....

....

....

....

....

The
SPIRITUAL PATH
is a
JOURNEY
into your
CREATIVE POWER
and
RESPONSIBILITY.

The Universal law of attraction brings like intentions—not like actions—together.

Whom Are You Attracting?

Take a moment to think about the people in your life. In general, are they people who . . .

- Please others so they feel better themselves?
- Gossip?
- Love life?
- Trust the Universe?
- Don't understand why things happen to them?
- Want revenge?
- Are angry and shout?
- Are angry and don't shout?
- Give freely?

Create your own list so you can see whom you are attracting.

....

....

....

....

....

....

....

Write here what you learn about yourself.

....

....

....

....

....

....

....

....

....

....

....

*M*ost people think that an intention is a goal. For example, an athlete intends to run her best race, a father intends to feed his family, and so on. But a goal is not an intention. It is an out-tention. What most people call intentions are actually out-tentions. An out-tention is the application of your will to accomplish a physical goal. An in-tention is the quality of consciousness you bring to an action. When you choose an out-tention, you choose a physical goal. When you choose an in-tention, you choose consciousness.

An
IN-TENTION
is
the quality of
CONSCIOUSNESS
you bring to
an
ACTION.

*Y*our in-tentions determine your experiences, whether or not you are
aware of your in-tentions. When you become aware of your in-tentions,
you can change your experiences by changing your in-tentions.

The Real Thing

Remember a time when you intended something good for someone and the out-
come was hurtful to you. For example, you gave a gift and your friend did not
acknowledge your gift, or your friend ignored you.

....

....

....

....

Notice what you are feeling in your solar plexus, chest, and throat areas as you
remember this experience.

....

....

....

....

Now ask yourself, "What was my real in-tention?"

....

....

....

....

Write what you discover here.

....

....

....

....

....

....

....

....

....

....

....

....

When your in-tentions are the intentions of your soul, you attract others who hold the same in-tentions. Even if your out-tentions are different, you will be drawn to each other. Like in-tentions attract.

The choice of in-tention is the fundamental choice.

My Out-tentions and In-tentions

Make a list of one or more of your top goals (out-tentions) for this year. Beside each goal, write your in-tention. Take some time to feel what your real in-tention is. It might be different than what you think at first.

Out-tention   Possible In-tentions

....

....

....

....

....

....

....

....

....

....

....

....

In writing, reflect on your discoveries.

....

....

....

....

....

....

....

....

....

....

....

....

....

....

....

....

....

Part 1 Bonus Exercises

Bonus Exercise 1

Make a list of the aspects of your life you most identify with, such as being a parent, a professional person, or a student; or your religion, culture, sex, history, and so forth. Consider each, one at a time. For the first part of the coming week, be aware of these aspects as you go through your day. Notice how you feel—what physical sensations you experience—when you are with people who are the same as you, and when you are with people who are different. Write your observations here.

....

....

....

....

....

....

....

....

For the second part of your week, imagine that the aspects you identify with have been taken away from you—that you are no longer a student, parent, woman, man, Catholic, Jew, American, lawyer, mother, or whatever. Notice what physical sensations you experience in your body as you imagine yourself without these aspects. How do your daily interactions change? Record your observations here.

....

....

....

....

....

....

....

....

Write what you discovered about yourself.

....

....

....

....

....

....

Bonus Exercise 2

The next time you have a choice to make, practice being a scientist of the soul. Follow these steps before you choose:

1. Visualize as clearly as you can what consequences the action you are considering is most likely to create. For example, if you feel angry and are about to shout, look at the consequences that shouting has created for you in the past (such as people avoiding you, fearing you, withdrawing from you, not being real with you, and so on).
2. Ask yourself if you want to create these consequences again.
3. Repeat the process with your next option.
4. When you have done this with each of your options, choose the one that will create the consequences you want to create.

Write what you discover here. (You can use this practice anytime, and especially when you are about to do or say something you are not sure about.)

....

....

....

....

....

....

....

....

PART 2

How to Choose

On a Personal Note
—Linda

As our friendship developed, Gary and I began to call each other spiritual buddies. My personal experience, however, was difficult and uncomfortable. The frightened parts of my personality seemed to be surfacing all the time. For example, I found that I wanted to please Gary so I would feel safe. If he did not respond the way I wanted him to, however, I would feel resentful or inferior, and tell him he should find someone else, someone who was worthy of him. Or I would react with anger if I thought he was acting superior. Or a jealous part of my personality would be activated, and I would withdraw without letting him know why.

All of these things, and many more, had happened in my previous relationships with men. This time, though, I made a real commitment to myself to look clearly at the frightened parts of my personality. Instead of blaming and judging Gary—and eventually leaving him to find the "right one"—I committed to healing these frightened parts.

I decided to be the "right one" for myself. This commitment was to my own spiritual growth, to creating authentic power rather than trying to change or criticize others when I reacted emotionally to them. For the first time, I began to challenge all the parts of my personality that wanted to please others so I could feel better, or that resented, blamed, judged, or felt superior or inferior—in other words, the frightened parts.

6

The Personality

Your personality is the part of you that was born at a certain time and will die at a certain time. It is also the part of you that becomes happy and sad, frightened and joyful, angry and caring. Your soul is the part of you that existed before you were born and will continue to exist after you die. Your personality is perfectly suited to the needs of your soul.

The Perfect Personality

Quickly list some physical characteristics you were born with and you do not like, but that you are willing to see from a different perspective. For example:

- I hate my thin/thick/curly/straight hair.
- I wish I weren't so short/tall.
- My poor vision keeps me from doing what I want.
- I wish my skin weren't white/black/yellow/brown.
- I don't like my brown/green/blue eyes.
- I can't sing on key.

When you have completed your list, go back to each item and say to yourself, "What if this part of my personality were perfectly suited for my journey through the Earth school?"

Now open yourself to the possibility that this is exactly the way it is. Write your reflections on the difference this possibility might make in your perceptions of your personality.

....

....

....

....

....

....

....

....

....

....

....

....

....

....

....

*Y*our intuition is the voice of the nonphysical world, and
your intuitional structure is the way you experience intuition.

How Do You Experience Intuition?

Can you recall ways you have, or may have, experienced intuition—for example, knowing when something is going to happen before it happens, knowing what someone is feeling or thinking before he or she tells you, or seeing significant meaning in ordinary circumstances?

Open yourself to ways you may be experiencing intuition that you haven't yet recognized.

Write what you find.

....

....

....

....

....

....

....

....

....

....

Intellect is the ability to think and reason based on data gathered by the five senses. Emotions are currents of energy that run through you, informing you about frightened and loving aspects of your personality. Your physical body, intuitional structure, intellect, emotions, five-sensory perceptions, and multisensory perceptions make up your personality.

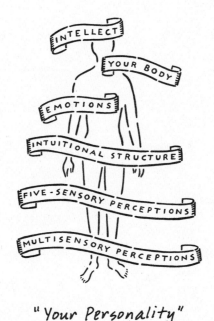

"Your Personality"

While you are under the control of frightened parts of your personality, you cannot give the gifts your soul wants to give.

Your Personality

Frightened parts	*Loving parts*
↓	↓
Need healing	*Are healthy*
↓	↓
Influence others with	*Create*

Appearance Intelligence	*Harmony Cooperation*
Strength Wealth Talents	*Sharing Reverence for Life*
Etc.	
↓	↓
In order to create	*In order to create*
External Power	*Authentic Power*
↓	↓
So they can	*So they can*
Feel safe, valuable, lovable	*Give gifts to Life*

Imagine your personality as a mansion with a different individual living in each room. Each has unique perceptions, values, and behaviors, and if you are not aware of the individuals, they do what they please.

Visiting Unexplored Rooms

Remember a time when . . .
- You disliked someone instantly.

....

....

....

....

....

- You intended to say something tender, but instead you said something hurtful.

....

....

....

....

....

....

- You ate to make yourself feel better.

....

....

....

....

- You felt close to someone and suddenly became offended by something he or she said.

....

....

....

....

Remember every detail you can. Think of that time as an experience of a frightened part of your personality that you did not know about and had an agenda of its own.

Decide if you want to continue being controlled by those parts of your personality. If not, say to yourself, "I have encountered a part of my personality that is frightened, and I have the ability to choose differently next time."

Notice and write your feelings.

....

....

....

....

....

Your compulsive, obsessive, and addictive behaviors each show you frightened parts of your personality. Kind, patient, generous, loving, and trusting behaviors are the parts of your personality that are aligned with the intentions of your soul. Creating authentic power requires going through your mansion, room by room, and meeting each individual.

7

Unconscious Choice

W hen someone "pushes your button," a frightened part of your personality becomes active, and you do things you regret. Becoming aware of the different parts of your personality allows you to choose for yourself what you will do in each circumstance.

PARTS
of your personality
that are
OUT OF CONTROL
=
BUTTONS
people can push.

*M*ost people can make good choices when they are calm
and grounded. Can you still make good choices when you are
jealous, vengeful, angry, feeling inferior, or feeling superior?

Name Your Parts

Name the parts, or aspects, of your personality you know are out of control.
Here's a clue: Look for any automatic emotional reactions, obsessive thoughts,
compulsive behaviors, or addictions.

Make a list here of those aspects.

....

....

....

....

....

....

....

*Y*ou may know you are angry, jealous, or resentful, but may
not realize that you are also feeling other things. Your obsessions,
compulsions, and addictions are also experiences of frightened
parts of your personality that you do not know about.

*U*ntil you come to terms with the different aspects of your personality, you will experience them only through the consequences they create, which are always painful.

Getting to Know Me

Refer to your list from the last exercise, Name Your Parts. Look at each part of your personality on your list, one at a time. As you consider each, say to yourself, "I am aware of you now, and I in-tend to remain aware of you while I make my choices."

Give yourself whatever time you need with each of these parts of your personality.

Record here your reflections and observations as you do this.

....

....

....

....

....

....

....

....

....

Each painful emotion and uncontrollable reaction is a reminder to look inside yourself, not outside yourself. There is no other way to meet the unconscious parts of your personality.

Searching for Unconscious Parts

During the next forty-eight hours, try this experiment: Whenever you react to anything, say to yourself, "I have encountered a frightened part of my personality." Notice what you reacted to and how you reacted. (You may want to make notes on a small notepad.)

Describe here what your experiment revealed to you.

....

....

....

....

....

....

....

....

....

....

....

There is no joy in the experiences of unconscious choices, and there is always pain. You will make unconscious choices until you bring the parts of your personality you do not know about into your awareness, examine them, and change them.

8
Conscious Choice

Conscious choices require awareness of in-tentions. Becoming familiar with all the parts of your personality, and knowing their in-tentions, allows you to choose among them, which puts you at the steering wheel.

You can take control of your decisions, just as a driver takes control of her car. You are no longer a passenger who is driven by one driver or another. Instead, you know where each of your passengers wants to go, but you choose where to drive them.

Driver or Passenger?

Remember an occasion when you were doing one thing while, at the same time, a part of your personality wanted to do something else. For example:

• You are at work, and all you can think of is going on vacation.
• You want to be loving to your spouse, but you are angry about what she said before breakfast.
• You love your sister, but you feel jealous, remembering how she used to get all of your parents' attention.
• You start a program you know will help you, but you keep thinking about what you would rather be doing.

Write about the occasion you have identified. Be specific.

....

....

....

....

....

....

....

....

....

....

With this experience clearly in mind, ask yourself:

- "Where do I really want to go?"

....

....

....

....

....

....

....

....

- "Where do the other parts of my personality want to go?"

....

....

....

....

....

....

....

....

Now make your choice.

*W*hen you are aware of what a part of your personality wants, but you choose otherwise, you make a conscious choice. That is how you become the force that changes your life.

Become the Force

The next time you find a frightened part of your personality (notice when you become angry, jealous, hold a grudge, etc.), follow these steps:

1. Stop.
2. Notice where you feel this frightened part of your personality in your body—where there are uncomfortable physical sensations, such as in your throat, chest, or solar plexus areas.
3. While you are feeling these uncomfortable sensations in your body, decide what you want to do.

Every time you use this practice, record here what you experienced and what you decided.

....

....

....

....

....

....

....

Your Guest List

Make a list of the aspects of your personality that you welcome and those you do not. Take your time. Consider, for example, the following:

Welcome Parts	*Unwelcome Parts*
Loving	Sloppy
Generous	Secretive
Playful	Jealous
Patient	Vengeful

Now, one by one, imagine welcoming them as though they were friends. Notice how you feel as you welcome each. Note especially the physical sensations in your solar plexus, chest, and throat areas.

Continue this practice until you begin to see all the parts of your personality as honored guests.

Imagine that you are at a large house party. Some of the guests are kind, some are angry, some are patient, some are jealous. Others are so rude you wonder how they got invited. The house represents your personality, and the guests are different parts of your personality.

*When you know
all the parts of your personality
you can place your*
WILL
between

THEIR IMPULSES

and

YOUR ACTIONS.

9

Responsible Choice

*E*very choice you make brings a different experience into being, and you cannot stop choosing. Therefore, you cannot stop creating. From the perspective of your soul, the choices you make are one with who and what you are.

People who do not understand the magnitude of their creative power, and do not use it consciously, see themselves as victims. Their attention is directed outward, finding faults, advantages, opportunities, failures, and successes.

A *creator experiments with his life.*

Which Trail Will You Choose?

List a few of your recent decisions. They can be decisions about what you chose to say to a friend when you were upset, as well as decisions about other activities.

....

....

....

....

....

Consider each one of your decisions as a choice of a trail. Think about other choices you could have made. Imagine these as trails you could have taken. Write your reflections on these choices.

....

....

....

....

....

....

....

In a larger sense, ask yourself if the trail you are on now is really the one you want to take. If so, describe why. If not, describe why not.

A victim blames others, judges friends, and pities herself. A creator is grateful for the lessons she learns. She sees that she alone is responsible for her choices.

I Am Responsible for My Choices

Say these words to yourself: "I am responsible for the choices I make and the consequences they create."

If you aren't ready to say these words with commitment, try an experiment. Say to yourself, "I am willing to look at the possibility that I am responsible for the choices I make and the consequences they create." Repeat this three times.

When you repeat these words, notice what physical sensations you feel in the areas of your throat, chest, and solar plexus. Describe what you are feeling here.

....

....

....

....

....

....

....

....

....

An unconscious choice is a reaction. A conscious choice is a response. When you choose a response that will create consequences for which you are willing to assume responsibility, you make a responsible choice.

You and Spiritual Growth

You can do this exercise alone or with a friend you trust. Say out loud, "I alone am responsible for my own spiritual growth." Repeat this several times.

Record here any changes you notice in your experiences.

....

....

....

....

....

....

....

....

....

....

....

Responsibility is not a burden you must carry, but a doorway to your freedom.

When you assume
RESPONSIBILITY
for your experiences, your life becomes
MEANINGFUL
and
you become capable of
RELATIONSHIPS
of substance and depth.

Responsible choice is the healing dynamic that removes the power of your fears from over you. It is the way to use your life as it was meant to be used—to align your personality with your soul.

10
Pulling It Together

$\mathcal{M}$ost people use their intellects when they make decisions, but as you become emotionally aware, you utilize your emotions, too. When you use your intuition, you also access the compassion and wisdom of nonphysical guides and teachers. Multisensory humans use all three sources of information—they put intellect in the service of intuition, and they consult their emotions.

Intuition

Can you remember a time when you knew you were making the right choice, and yet you were very frightened to do it? If so, let yourself relive this experience in your imagination. Notice what physical sensations you are having in your throat, chest, and solar plexus areas. Describe here what happened and what you are now experiencing.

....

....

....

....

....

....

....

....

....

....

....

....

....

Now remember your inner sense of having made the right choice. Let yourself become familiar with your own way of experiencing intuition. Try to put it into words here.

....

....

....

....

....

....

....

....

....

....

....

....

Your intellect and emotions may lead you in one direction, while your intuition shows you another. Which is more important to you: getting what you think you want, or feeling good about what you do?

Did It, Anyway

Can you remember a time when you didn't want to do something and you did it, anyway, because you knew it was the right thing to do?

Describe it here.

....

....

....

....

....

What did your intellect tell you?

....

....

....

What feelings did you have?

....

....

....

What was your intuition showing you?

....

....

....

11
Internal Landscape

*Y*ou travel simultaneously through two landscapes—your external landscape and your internal landscape. Your external landscape may be appealing, but if your internal landscape is not also appealing, you will not be happy.

If you take the time to look, you can know in advance what internal landscape your choice will create. Take a test drive. Explore the internal landscape you encounter when you consider first one option, then another, and then yet another. The thought of each option—such as moving, marrying, or changing jobs—creates experiences inside you. Just thinking about the possibility changes your internal landscape.

Take a Test-drive

Test-drive a possible future with your emotions and your intuition. See how you feel when you think about each of your possible futures, one at a time. For example:

- If you are ending a relationship, you may feel pain in your chest and solar plexus areas (fearful emotions) and know that breaking up is the best choice for you (intuition).
- If you are thinking about changing jobs, you may feel open and relaxed in your chest, solar plexus, and throat areas (trusting emotions) and know the new job is the best choice for you (intuition).
- If you are thinking about getting married, you may feel open and relaxed in your chest area (trusting emotions), tightness in your solar plexus area (fearful emotions), and know that getting married is not the best choice for you.

Decide here which possible future you will bring into your life.

....

....

....

....

....

*Y*ou do not have to dive into the water to see how it feels. You can put your toe in first by thinking about a possibility and, at the same time, paying attention to what you experience inside. Do that with each option you can imagine, and then make your choice. Create the internal landscape that is the most nurturing, healing, creative, and joyful for you.

Put Your Toe in First

For the next few days, try the following experiment. Before you make a choice that stretches you (for example, not "What flavor ice cream will I eat?" but "Is eating this ice cream the healthiest choice for me?"), consider each possible option you have. Do this without the energy of commitment. Just preview each option by . . .

1. Thinking about it (intellect).
2. Feeling the physical sensations in your solar plexus, chest, and throat areas (emotional awareness).
3. Seeing how you feel inside about choosing the option (intuition).

Then choose.

Write your discoveries here.

....

....

....

....

....

....

....

Responsible choice is choosing the harvest before you plant the crop.

Part 2 Bonus Exercises

Bonus Exercise 1

Part One: For the next forty-eight hours, every time you react, ask yourself, "What is my in-tention?" For example, when you are impatient, defensive, in a power struggle, or angry, stop in that moment to examine yourself by asking, "What is my in-tention?" In other words, what lies behind your impatience, defensiveness, anger, or the power struggle?

Carry a small notepad with you and write your reactions and intentions. Write your most significant discoveries here.

....

....

....

....

....

....

....

....

....

....

Part Two: Consider the choices you made and the actions you took during the last forty-eight hours. Try to distinguish between your out-tention (what you are going to do) and your in-tention (why you are going to do it) in each instance.

Write here what you learned.

....

....

....

....

....

....

....

....

....

....

....

....

....

Bonus Exercise 2

Try this experiment for the next week. Think of at least three areas in your life right now to which you react and would like to be able to see differently—for example, a person you don't like and whom you have been blaming or judging, or a job situation you find so unacceptable that it is hard for you to go to work each morning.

For this experiment to work, it is important that you allow yourself to imagine that your reactions are showing you something that you need to learn about yourself.

Every morning, set your in-tention to see this person or situation differently. At night, give yourself some reflective time to become aware of possible changes in the way that you are seeing this person or situation and yourself. Be patient with yourself.

Write what you discover. If you need to, take more than a week with this experiment.

HOW TO CHOOSE

PART 3

Power

On a Personal Note
—Gary

I didn't know anything about spirituality when I wrote my first book, *The Dancing Wu Li Masters: An Overview of the New Physics,* and so I didn't think about it at all. Instead, I thought about how unjust and brutal the world was, how unappreciated I was, and how I would pay my rent, buy food, and find sex. In other words, I was an angry, bitter, unproductive, and judgmental sex addict.

That was my condition when I was invited to a weekly meeting of physicists at the Lawrence Berkeley Laboratory in Berkeley, California. I went to that meeting out of curiosity. I left fascinated. The physicists there discussed the deepest questions I could imagine, questions such as "Does consciousness create reality?"

When I returned home, I discovered to my surprise that I could not reproduce the discussions that had so stimulated me. I began to read about quantum physics, and I questioned the physicists I was meeting. Slowly I began to understand the fundamental concepts of quantum mechanics, such as "complementarity," the "uncertainty principle," and the "wave-particle duality."

I decided to write a book based on my research as a gift to those who would later become interested in physics. I hoped they would benefit from my efforts by reading one volume instead of spending days in a physics library and hours talking with physicists. While I was writing this book, I forgot to be angry, judgmental, and frightened, and I forgot about my need for sex. Writing the book excited me more than any of those things, but when I stopped working on the book, all of them returned.

Within six months, I noticed that *The Dancing Wu Li Masters* had taken on a life of its own, and that it was wiser, funnier, and more patient than I was. I had written each chapter as I felt moved, regardless of what I had put into the outline beforehand. In retrospect, I was amazed to discover that chapters written months apart fit together perfectly. My life was so painful when I was not writing the book, and so fulfilling and engaging when I was, that I decided I wanted to live my life as my book was being written—spontaneously, intelligently, and joyfully.

I am grateful that I followed my heart, excitement, and joy instead of my fears, and that I chose to write *The Dancing Wu Li Masters*. That choice created possibilities, and yet more choices, that would not have been available to me otherwise.

12

Authentic Power

*I*n order to understand authentic power, you must understand that you have an immortal soul. Your personality is a tool of your soul, but it is not separate from your soul. The choices you make while you are on the Earth create consequences which, if they do not occur before you die, will occur afterward.

The lessons your soul wants to learn arrive in the form of your experiences. When you decide to change, you learn from your painful experiences, because you do not want to create them again. If you do not learn, you do not change.

When you align your personality with your soul, you bring meaning, purpose, joy, and fulfillment into your life. People and the Earth become important to you, and your activities have value to you.

When you align your
PERSONALITY
with your
SOUL
you
create

Purpose   Meaning   Gratitude   Fulfillment
Connection to people   Connection to Life

Transforming the frightened parts of your personality requires your choice, because they will change only when you choose to change them.

Really Learning

Remember an occasion when you were very upset, angry, shocked, or deeply felt a loss. If it helps, close your eyes. While you are reliving this experience, remember how you acted. Did you cry, rage, withdraw, feel confused, or become depressed? What physical sensations are you feeling in your throat, chest, and solar plexus areas? What actions did you take?

Now go back to the beginning of this experience in your imagination. This time, let yourself feel the physical sensations in your body that you felt before you took any action.

Say to yourself, "I in-tend to learn everything I can from this experience." Close your eyes and open yourself to learning. Give yourself some time. Then begin to pay attention to your life—to what people say to you, what you overhear, signs you see, and dreams you have.

Write what you discover.

....

....

....

....

....

....

....

*A*uthentic power is your potential, but you must bring that potential into your life. You do that by healing the painful parts of your personality, and cultivating the joyful and grateful parts.

Your soul
wants to learn
a lesson
of
WISDOM
RESPONSIBILITY
POWER
or
LOVE.

---

*W*hen you transform the frightened parts of your personality into parts that create with the intentions of your soul, the energy of your soul flows effortlessly into your life, and you become whole, healthy, and inwardly secure.

13

Creating Authentic Power

You can use your will to make choices that empower you rather than disempower you. You can also make choices that create consequences for which you are willing to assume responsibility, even while you are feeling angry, jealous, etc. When you do that, you draw strength from your choices instead of losing power because of them.

The creation of authentic power is self-transformation—through the use of your will—from a victim of your experiences to the creator of them.

My Will

As before, remember a time when you had a painful emotional reaction—for example, you became very upset, withdrew and cried, raged at people, walked around confused for days, or became depressed. Really get back into that experience—feel it again.

But, this time, you get to make a new choice. Go through the same experience in your imagination again and consciously choose one of the following:

- React the same way again.
- Feel the sensations in your body without acting.
- Feel the sensations in your body and act with one of the intentions of your soul: harmony, cooperation, sharing, or reverence for Life.

Describe the experience and what you chose here.

....

....

....

....

....

....

*W*hen you challenge a frightened part of your personality,
it loses power over you and you gain power over it.

Change That Part

Pick a part of your personality you would like to change. For example, your . . .

- Anger
- Jealousy
- Resentment
- Judgment
- Anxiety
- Power struggles with your spouse, children, friend, etc.

Set your in-tention to heal this part of your personality. Watch when this part becomes active. When it does, challenge it by not doing what you usually do. While you are feeling painful sensations in your body, decide how you will act. If you chose words and actions that create consequences for which you are willing to assume responsibility, congratulate yourself.

Write your in-tention here.

....

....

....

....

....

*A*uthentic power does not come to those who talk about it, read about it, meditate on it, or pray for it. It comes to those who earn it.

Authentic power is using your will
to transform your life.

FROM	$\longrightarrow$	TO
Experience	$\longrightarrow$	Experiment
Victim	$\longrightarrow$	Creator
Theory	$\longrightarrow$	Meaning

---

*W*hen you have the courage to feel what you are feeling rather than act in fear, and then choose the intentions of your soul, you create authentic power.

14
Attention

Multisensory humans see themselves as souls, even while they interact, work, and raise children. Their goal is authentic power, and their potential is a planet of Universal Humans: citizens of the Universe whose allegiance is to Life.

The transformation of human consciousness from five-sensory to multisensory is happening from the inside out. Old challenges no longer appeal, and millions of individuals are finding new interests and new goals. There is no place on the Earth where it is not happening.

How Are You Becoming Multisensory?

List the ways you have discovered that you are more than five-sensory. For example, I am . . .

- Using this journal.
- Interested in my in-tentions.
- Suspecting/sensing that I am more than a mind and body.
- Becoming intuitive.
- Discovering meaning in ordinary experiences.

- _____
- _____
- _____
- _____
- _____
- _____
- _____
- _____
- _____
- _____
- _____
- _____
- _____

*M*ultisensory perception is not new—in fact, most religions are named after multisensory humans—but never before has humanity as a whole experienced this transformation.

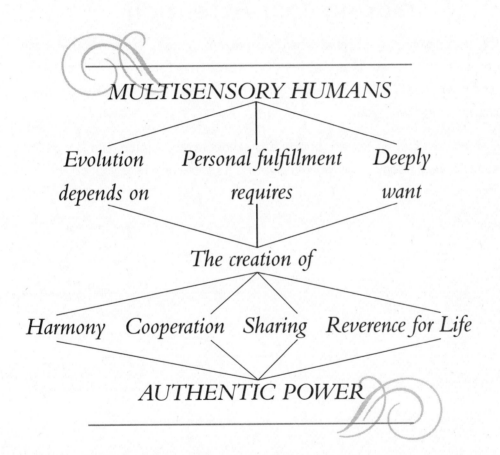

MULTISENSORY HUMANS

Evolution depends on · Personal fulfillment requires · Deeply want

The creation of

Harmony · Cooperation · Sharing · Reverence for Life

AUTHENTIC POWER

*M*ultisensory perception is exploding into the human experience, and with it the understanding of power as the alignment of the personality with the soul.

*W*hen you focus on what nurtures, sustains, and feeds you, you gain power.

Tracking Your Attention

For the next day or two, observe where your attention goes. Note whether it is focused on thoughts, words, and actions that come from fear and doubt, or from love and trust. This will take some discipline. It will help if you carry this Journal or a small notepad with you.

As much as possible, write very briefly each thought you notice, and beside it write *love* or *fear.* Keeping this log will give you a sample of where your attention is going.

Thought   Love or Fear?

....

....

....

....

....

....

....

....

*W*hen you choose in fear and doubt, you lose power, and
when you choose in love and trust, you gain power. You challenge the frightened parts of your personality by choosing where
you will put your attention.

Soul Perspective

Remember a painful event that you still feel was unfair, but that you would now
like to understand in a different way.

For this practice, assume the Universe is wise and compassionate.
Ask yourself:

1) "Why would a compassionate and wise Universe help me create this experience?"

....

....

....

2) "What have I gained—what strengths have I developed, or could I develop—
from this experience?"

....

....

....

....

Open yourself to answers, and remain open until they come. They may not come
immediately, or in ways you expect.

When you ask, "Why me?" without self-pity, you open yourself to the perspective of your soul.

When you ask, "Why me?" with self-blame and judgment of others, you invoke the least powerful and most painful parts of your personality.

Where Your Attention Goes

Do this practice in real time. Notice the next time you encounter something that always makes you irritated, impatient, angry, judgmental, jealous, etc. For example:

• When I am in a long line at the bank, I get angry.
• My spouse is never ready on time and I always get irritated and impatient.

Think about how you could respond differently. Then choose how you will respond.

Consider this experiment each time the occasion arises. Write here what you learned when you responded differently.

....

....

....

....

....

....

In order to choose where you will focus your attention next, you must know where it is now.

Experiment With Your Attention

Try this practice from time to time:

- Experience where you are now.
- Move your attention to where you want it to go.
- Experience that new place.
- Decide how long you will stay there.

Keep notes here on your experiences.

....

....

....

....

....

....

....

....

....

....

....

15
How to Challenge

You challenge a frightened part of your personality by allowing yourself to feel it fully, and *while you are feeling it fully,* choose not to act in jealousy, fear, and so forth. Similarly, you challenge your jealousy by allowing yourself to feel it fully, and *while you are feeling it fully,* choose not to act jealously. You can challenge any painful emotion this way—allow yourself to experience it as fully as you can, and while you are experiencing it, choose not to speak or act on what you feel.

*Y*ou *do not need someone to remind you to shift your attention, change your in-tention, and try something else. You can remember that yourself when you feel a painful emotion.*

Shift Your Attention

For the next twenty-four hours, when you feel emotions that are painful to you, such as anger, jealousy, sadness, fear, etc., remember to shift your attention, change your in-tention, and try something else.

Write your significant discoveries here.

....

....

....

....

....

....

....

....

....

....

A challenge is an in-tention to change yourself for the better. You use your will to reshape your personality. When you do that, you reshape your experience.

Challenge It

Select an aspect of your personality that is frightened—in other words, a part that is angry, sad, disappointed, jealous, etc., that you would like to change. Record it here.

....

Each time this part of your personality returns, notice what physical sensations you feel in your throat, chest, and solar plexus areas. Describe them here.

....

....

....

Ask yourself, "What would be the most constructive response I could choose?" Reflect on the possibilities here.

....

....

....

....

....

Keep a log of your progress.

....

....

....

....

....

....

....

....

....

....

....

....

....

....

....

....

Credit your progress for even small steps. For example, when you notice you are angry and stop to feel the sensations in your body, even for a few seconds, before you create your usual reaction, celebrate your awareness and in-tention to change.

16
Authentic Needs

*Y*our sense of meaning, like a compass needle, always points in the direction your soul wants to go. The more closely you follow it, the more meaning you experience. The more you ignore it, the more that meaning drains from your life.

*Y*our internal compass can help you distinguish authentic needs from artificial needs. Authentic needs are the needs of your soul.

AUTHENTIC NEEDS	ARTIFICIAL NEEDS
Needs of the soul	*Needs of the personality*
Align personality and soul	*Manipulate and control*
Creativity serves the soul	*Envy creativity of others*
Love and be loved	*Strive to be safe and valuable*
Life fills with meaning	*Life empties of meaning*
Create healing, constructive consequences	*Create painful, destructive consequences*
Give gifts of the soul	*Insist on being right*
Fear disappears	*Life filled with fear*
Attract others who pursue authentic needs	*Attract others who pursue artificial needs*
Create authentic power	*Create external power*

*A*rtificial needs come from the frightened parts of your personality. You feel powerless, and instead of addressing the issue directly, you create a need to address it for you. This is the pursuit of external power.

Authentic Need or Artificial Need?

Remember the last few times you had a painful emotional reaction. It may have been a power struggle with your spouse or child or friend, anger at a slow driver, impatience with a long line at the grocery store, disapproval of some food you were served, etc.

Describe each circumstance briefly here. Look closely at what you wanted, or thought you needed, in each situation. Now consider each item on your list and ask yourself if that need was 1) an authentic need or 2) an artificial need.

Reaction	1	2

When you pursue authentic needs, your life becomes meaningful, but when you are satisfying artificial needs, your life becomes empty, and that is how using your inner compass can help you distinguish between the two.

Reassessment

Make a list of some things you would like, for example:

- A new car
- A meaningful job
- A thoughtful spouse
- A child

Review each, one at a time, and ask yourself, "Is this a need of 1) my soul or 2) my personality?" Indicate with a checkmark.

Things You Would Like	1	2
....	....	....
....	....	....
....	....	....
....	....	....
....	....	....
....	....	....
....	....	....
....	....	....

Now make a list of things you have that are most important to you, such as . . .

- My values
- My children
- My wardrobe

Review each of these and ask yourself, "Is this a need of 1) my soul or 2) my personality?" Indicate with a checkmark.

Things Most Important	1	2

What did you learn about yourself?

*T*o create authentic power, you must use your painful experiences as they were meant to be used: to discover what you need to heal inside yourself.

Painful emotions
are signals
from your soul
that remind you to
STOP
and
EXPERIENCE
what you are feeling.

*W*hen you can recognize the difference between your authentic needs and your artificial needs, you will develop a natural give-and-take and become more flexible.

The behavior of others is never an issue in your spiritual growth, but your emotional reaction always is.

I'm Sure It Is You

Think of someone you don't like. Identify exactly what you dislike. For example:

- Her stinginess
- His loud boasting
- Her lack of integrity

Note these characteristics in your journal. Be specific. Now look within yourself to find the same characteristics.

Be patient with yourself. This may take some time. Write what you learn about yourself here.

....

....

....

....

....

....

....

....

GIVING AND RECEIVING LOVE

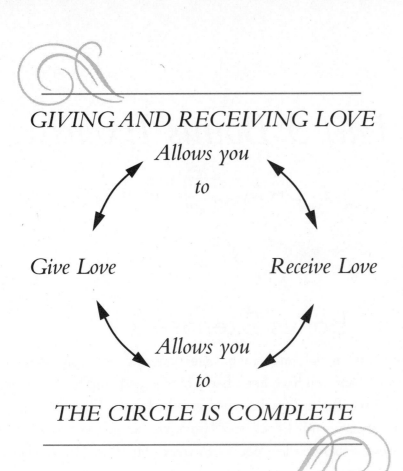

Allows you

to

Give Love   Receive Love

Allows you

to

THE CIRCLE IS COMPLETE

Y*our purpose on the Earth is to become a personality that creates with the intentions of your soul.*

The intentions of your soul are harmony, cooperation, sharing, and reverence for Life.

Part 3 Bonus Exercises

Bonus Exercise 1

Picture yourself with a deformed face—unrecognizable and ugly when you look in a mirror. Perhaps you have been badly burned and your face is covered with purple scar tissue. Perhaps you have had a stroke and you drool from a corner of your limp, misshapen mouth. People recoil from you, but you are still you. How do you feel? How would you like people to treat you? Can you do that for others?

Write what you learned.

....

....

....

....

....

....

Bonus Exercise 2

What actions do you want to take (or you say you want to take), but either lack the courage to take or have been avoiding? For example, you need to talk to a family member about a difficult situation but have been putting it off, or you want a raise but you haven't asked for it.

Say to yourself, "(The action you have not taken) is my out-tention. What is my in-tention?" For example, "Am I judging someone because I want to be right, or am I not asking for a raise because I don't feel worthy?" Now decide if you want to keep your intention or choose another.

Write what you learn.

....

....

....

....

....

....

....

....

....

....

Continue this exercise for a month. Write here what you discover each time you identify an in-tention you do not want to keep and then change it.

PART 4

Choice and Power

On a Personal Note
—Linda

For most of my life, I thought that harmony was the absence of conflict, so I did everything I could to make sure there was no conflict around me. If I felt disharmony inside, I would distract myself from those uncomfortable feelings. If I perceived a lack of harmony around me, I would do everything I could to restore the harmony, so I was frequently trying to please other people.

As I began to experiment with creating harmony, I realized that what I needed to do or say was quite different from what I had done in the past. For example, if I feel disharmony now, I allow myself (when I am balanced) to put my attention on any physical sensations in my body, especially in the areas of my throat, chest, and solar plexus. Instead of trying to distract myself, I consciously choose what I want to do or say, while I am feeling the discomfort.

An example of this occurred several months after I met Gary, as our friendship was deepening. I knew I had something to tell him about myself that I was sure would end our relationship. I did not want to tell him or to end our relationship, but if I wanted integrity with myself and him, I needed to.

I still remember how scared I felt when I finally spoke, and how loving and compassionate he was. He knew how difficult I found it to tell him those things. I realized that by saying exactly what I needed to say, but was most frightened to say to Gary, I truly created harmony. I told the truth, and I was willing to accept the consequences.

Since then, we continue to share the things we most don't want to speak about. We know that whatever we leave unsaid will eventually end our spiritual partnership and prevent the creation of harmony.

17
Harmony

$\mathcal{I}$n order to create harmony with another person, you must care enough about that person to hear his story, share her struggles, and be with her while the parts of her personality that are frightened come to the surface. It is easy to create harmony with someone who cares for you, but it is difficult when that person is angry, disdainful, or judgmental.

Real Harmony?

Remember a time when you were in a difficult situation with another person. Did you create harmony? Ask yourself these questions:

- Did I say or do something to make that person feel better, even though it wasn't true?
- Did I do something so I could feel better about myself?
- Was my feeling of well-being dependent on that person's agreement with me?

Note here what you discovered about yourself and about harmony.

....

....

....

....

....

....

....

....

....

....

....

....

....

*H*armony requires integrity. You cannot control whether other people are authentic, but you can decide whether or not you *will be.*

Your soul
wants HARMONY
with those you consider
YOUR FRIENDS
and with those you consider
YOUR ENEMIES.

*H*armony with another is not always possible, but the in-tention to create it is.

*T*he parts of your personality that object to harmony object
also to your spiritual growth.

Friendship and Harmony

When you find yourself in an uncomfortable situation with a friend, ask yourself
these questions to see if harmony is really what you want to create:

- Am I doing or saying something to make my friend feel better, even though it isn't true?
- Am I doing or saying something so I can feel better about myself?
- Does my feeling of well-being depend on my friend's agreement with me?
- If my friend becomes angry and won't speak to me, will I still feel that my in-tention is to create harmony?

Write here what you discover.

....

....

....

....

....

....

....

....

Harmony is the conscious creation of a loving world.

Spiritual Activism

When you interact with those who disagree, especially those with whom you very much disagree, ask yourself:

- Are my in-tentions to manipulate, or to create harmony?
- Do I revere my adversary as much as my ally?
- Am I making anyone a villain?
- Am I opposing people instead of behaviors or policies?

Describe a recent instance when you interacted with someone with whom you disagree.

....

....

....

....

....

....

Was your in-tention to manipulate, or to create harmony? ....

Do you revere this person as you would an ally? ....

Do you make this person a villain? ....

Do you oppose the person or the behaviors or policies? ....

18
Cooperation

In every collective endeavor, individuals assemble in the service of a common goal and cooperate to accomplish it. This is the five-sensory understanding of cooperation: the coordination of efforts to accomplish a common goal. Multisensory humans strive to create authentic power—to align their personalities with their souls. They do not need the cooperation of others to accomplish that, and others do not need their cooperation to create authentic power.

The pursuit of authentic power is not a collective endeavor. Your spiritual path is for you alone to walk, and the spiritual paths of others are for them to walk, because each has his work to do, and only you can do yours.

Multisensory humans
know their goal
is not
as important as
HOW
they accomplish it.

The goal of multisensory humans is spiritual growth. Multisensory humans bring emotional awareness, responsible choice, intuition, trust in the Universe, and their in-tention to create authentic power to their common endeavors.

19
Cocreation

Multisensory humans cooperate to contribute to Life and to create experiences that are worthy of their time on the Earth. This type of cooperation is a cocreation. It inspires all, harms none, is deeply satisfying, and requires from each the in-tention to create authentic power.

Multisensory
COOPERATION
requires the
IN-TENTION
to create
AUTHENTIC POWER.

Y ou can resent, judge, and envy colleagues while cooperating with them, but you cannot cocreate with them until you appreciate them as fellow souls.

Cooperating

This is an experiment to do with someone who is important to you. Let the other person know that you are experimenting with how to cooperate and would like to invite him or her to be your special friend to experiment with.

Make an appointment to do something together that is meaningful to both of you. For example:

- Clean out places of unconsciousness in each other's homes together.
- Volunteer for meaningful work in your community.
- Enjoy nature.
- Go somewhere neither of you has been before.
- Help a friend or elderly person with something he or she needs.

Allow sufficient uninterrupted time together. Set your in-tention to cocreate this activity with your friend. Your goal is not simply to complete the task, but to use your time together consciously to grow spiritually.

Notice what choices you make and the in-tentions behind your choices. Use the following two pages to write what you discover.

Write your discoveries about cooperation and spiritual growth in your journal. Did you forget now and then that you were experimenting? What did you learn about yourself?

Cocreation requires the courage to examine and change yourself. Multisensory humans choose their goals, but they also choose their colleagues.

When you
COMPETE
you plant the seed of
WAR.
When you
COCREATE
you plant the seed of
PEACE.

Cocreators know their creative power, intend to use it wisely, and take responsibility for their creations.

Am I Competing?

Ask yourself (circle yes or no):

- Do I get jealous when others are invited to a party and I am not? Y / N
- Do I feel superior to people who don't have as much as I do? Y / N
- Do I get pouty when others get more attention? Y / N
- Do I always have to win (or won't play unless I can)? Y / N
- Do I feel I more valuable or less valuable than others? Y / N
- Do I have to have the last word? Y / N
- Do I argue frequently? Y / N

If you answered yes to any of the above, parts of your personality are competing.

Think of similar questions to ask yourself, and write your responses here.

....

....

....

....

....

....

....

Until you create authentic power, winning will be important to you.

COOPERATION VS. COCREATION

Five-sensory Cooperation	*Multisensory Cooperation*
Pursue external power	Create authentic power
Goal most important	People most important
See colleagues as coworkers	See colleagues as souls
Work to achieve goal	Learn about self

Cocreation is the conscious contribution of creativity and effort toward a common goal with the in-tention to grow spiritually in the process.

Cooperate for a Day

Think about how you can cooperate with others today. For example:
Use what you are doing with others as an opportunity to learn about yourself.
Notice your reactions, such as anger, resentment, jealousy, and judgment.
As you interact, ask yourself:

- What is my in-tention?
- Am I creating cooperation or am I competing?
- Am I cooperating to feel better about myself, or to please someone else?
- Is my desire to cocreate?
- Am I interested in the people I am with as much as in what I am doing?

Write here what you discover about yourself.

....

....

....

....

....

....

....

....

....

20
Sharing

*E*ven for ten thousand ounces of gold
I would not sell the way,
But I will give it for free right at the crossroad
If you can hear my sound.

Can you give what is precious to you? How often do you share the best that you have? What is the best that you have? What you share is important, but why you share it is even more important. Sharing is a deeper dynamic. It requires knowing your in-tentions.

When expectations accompany your gift, you pursue external power—your gift is a means to an end, and the end is for you, not the one who receives the gift.

Strings Attached

Remember a time when you gave a gift and you were upset at the response you received. Go back to that experience in your memory. Notice what physical sensations you feel in your solar plexus, chest, and throat areas. If the sensations are not immediately apparent, keep looking for them.

Describe the situation here and answer these questions:

- What was my intention in giving this gift?
- Was it truly a gift?
- Did I have a hidden agenda?

If you do not know all of your in-tentions before you share, you will discover them after you share, because you will become disappointed, or angry, or in other ways upset if your gift is thrown away or not appreciated.

A Real Gift?

Before you give a gift, ask yourself these questions:

- Do I expect my gift to be appreciated?
- Do I expect to be recognized?
- Do I feel that the person to whom I give my gift owes me in some way?
- What would I feel if the person who received my gift gave it away? Threw it away? Didn't like it?
- What is my in-tention for giving this gift?

Write here what you discover.

....

....

....

....

....

....

....

....

The more you need people to agree with you, the less open you are to what they think, feel, and believe. You are not truly sharing with them because you are trying to change them, and they cannot share with you because you are not listening.

Are You Really Sharing?

What is so important to you that you need to share information about it frequently? For example:

- Your diet
- How you exercise
- The way your boss is wrong
- Your political beliefs

List here what you need to share frequently.

....

....

....

....

....

....

....

....

What are you certain you are right about? For example:

- Your political beliefs
- Your religious beliefs
- Your economic beliefs
- Your understanding of a certain subject

....

....

....

....

....

How do you feel if others don't accept what you say or believe?

....

....

....

....

....

Write here what you learned about yourself and sharing.

....

....

....

....

....

21

The Greatest Gift

The parts of your personality that are frightened hoard anything they feel will benefit themselves, whether it is knowledge, affection, spare parts, or food. The scarcity they fear is not in their future, but in their present. It surrounds them, and they continually react to it. The solution is not to increase your accumulation, but to assess more accurately what you need.

Scarcity of
SELF-VALUE
cannot be remedied
by
Money
Recognition
Affection
Attention
or
Influence.

*W*hen scarcity exists for you internally, external abundance will not fill it, because the scarcity that creates the need to hoard is a scarcity of self-value.

When Do You Have Enough?

In what areas of your life do you feel a scarcity? For example, do you feel a shortage of any of the following:

- Time
- Friends
- Talent
- Good looks
- Money
- Love
- Attention

Make a list of what you don't have enough of.

....

....

....

....

....

....

Circle the items on your list that you are willing to look at from a new perspective. Consider each, and as you do:

- Notice any thoughts you have about how you don't have enough.
- Notice any painful sensations in your body, such as tight shoulders, clenched jaws, upset stomach, or pain in your chest.
- Ask yourself, "Am I willing to open to the possibility that it is my self-value that is lacking, and not what I at first think is lacking?"
- If yes, set the in-tention to heal the frightened parts of your personality that feel they don't have enough, and consider the possibility that you are valuable, loved, and internally abundant.

Do you feel you are developing a new perspective? Keep a log here of what changes you notice in yourself.

....

....

....

....

....

....

....

....

....

....

....

....

Internal abundance is realizing that you are worthy of your life, recognizing the potential for spiritual growth that your struggles offer you, and trusting the Universe.

The greatest
gift
you can give
is
your
presence.

Even when you are frightened of what you must do to share, you are grateful for the opportunity, because sharing energizes and fulfills you.

22
Reverence for Life

When you experience reverence, you see beyond appearances, your judgments disappear, and your heart opens. In other words, your attention goes to the essence of a person or thing and appearances become no more than costumes.

Can You See Differently?

Think of a person you know with whom you don't feel close but would like to. Why do you feel distant? Do you feel inferior or fearful, or envious of your friend, or disdainful, superior, and judgmental?

Then ask yourself (yes or no):

- Have I been looking only at my friend's Earth suit?..
- Have I been focusing on what he does?...
- Have I been focusing on how she dresses?..
- Do I feel I cannot communicate because of a misunderstanding or disagreement?..
- Am I distant because my life has taken me in a different direction?........................

Take whatever time you need on this exercise:

- Close your eyes and picture your friend.
- Set your in-tention to see beyond your friend's Earth suit.
- Remind yourself that you don't know all that goes into his life—his challenges, fears, joys, and terror.
- Remember that you are a soul, and your friend is a soul, also.

Open your eyes and notice how you feel about your friend now. Do you feel compassion? If not, continue this exercise until you feel a shift from seeing your friend only as a personality to knowing he is a soul wearing an Earth suit. Allow yourself to feel the instant that your fearful and judgmental reactions disappear and reverence appears.

Write your reflections here.

CHOICE AND POWER

The essence of who you are is your soul. Your personality is the costume your soul is wearing. Reverence is seeing the soul that is wearing the costume.

Deeper than Appearance

For this exercise, pick a day when you will be seeing many people—maybe those you know at work, some you may have met at a party, or many who are complete strangers in a restaurant, airport, or shopping center. Your assignment is to try to see each person as a soul instead of a personality. This is an inner experience. While you are doing this experiment, ask yourself:

- How am I feeling about each person?
- Am I remembering that each person is wearing an Earth suit that is perfect for him?
- Do the people that I see differently respond to me differently?
- If I interact, does my conversation with them have a different quality?

Write your experiences here.

_____

_____

_____

_____

_____

_____

Appearances always differ, but when you see the essence beneath appearances, your judgments disappear, and you create a world in which harm is not possible, because your relationships become soul-to-soul.

Holiness

When you wake tomorrow morning, say to yourself, "I intend to see holiness in every person and every thing today."

Think about what that might mean. If you forget during the day, remind yourself and set the in-tention again.

Write your experiences in your notepad as the day progresses and list your significant discoveries here.

....

....

....

....

....

When you become aware of yourself as a soul in the Earth school, you become aware of others as souls, too, and their personalities become interesting, just as different clothing is interesting.

My Earth Suit

Draw a picture of your own Earth suit. Take your time to put in every detail you can. Don't worry if you think you can't draw. This picture is for you. If you don't want to draw a picture, find a photo of yourself. Keep your drawing or photo as a reminder that your Earth suit was picked by your soul for your journey through the Earth school, and that it is perfect for you. (If this page isn't big enough, use a larger piece of paper.)

Part 4 Bonus Exercises

Bonus Exercise 1

Experiment with putting your intellect in the service of your heart this week by asking yourself before you speak or act, "If I follow my impulse, will I . . ."

- Create with an intention of my soul?
- Make myself more loving?
- Make myself more whole?

Write what you discover. Be specific.

....

....

....

....

....

....

....

Bonus Exercise 2

Choose an intention of your soul. (The intentions of your soul are harmony, cooperation, sharing, and reverence for life.) During the next week, keep your attention focused on the intention of the soul that you have chosen. Open yourself to the deeper meanings of this intention. As you discover deeper meanings of this intention, notice how it affects your experiences.

Write your discoveries.

....

....

....

....

....

....

....

....

....

....

....

....

....

PART 5

Responsible Choice

On a Personal Note
—Gary

The Dancing Wu Li Masters: An Overview of the New Physics was so well received that it surprised everyone. It got a rave review in the *New York Times,* was reprinted by every book club, and was translated into sixteen languages. It still sells around the world. As a result, I acquired a reputation as a popularizer of modern science, and people expected me to write more books on the subject.

I wanted to do that, so I began a three-volume series called *Physics and Consciousness.* This time, however, my intention was not to give a gift but to win a Pulitzer Prize. I wrote for years, and some of the chapters I wrote were fascinating. Yet the quality of my writing slowly declined until it appealed not even to me. The series had become a burden to me and did not satisfy at all. In fact, my life began to feel meaningless.

This experience could not have differed more from the one I had while writing *The Dancing Wu Li Masters.* Only later did I realize that writing *The Dancing Wu Li Masters* was an experience of authentic power—the alignment of my personality with my soul—while writing *Physics and Consciousness* was a pursuit of another kind of power—external power. I wrote *The Dancing Wu Li Masters* to give a gift. I wrote *Physics and Consciousness* to make myself feel worthy. I felt that people would appreciate, admire, and accept me if I won a valued prize.

Understanding the difference between authentic power and external power was the first step in freeing myself from my fantasies. It put me on a path that led to *The Seat of the Soul,* a book about the living, compassionate, wise Universe, and our role in it. In turn, that led me to Linda Francis, this Journal, and you.

23

The Inside Story

When you look inside, what you discover are the very things you find most repulsive in others. When you struggle against them in others, you have no chance of healing them in yourself. The more you struggle, the stronger they become, because ignoring them only feeds them and allows them to grow.

*W*hat you refuse to acknowledge in yourself begins to fill your thoughts and fantasies. That is a temptation.

What Are You Tempted By?

- To keep the extra money you are given by mistake?
- To have an affair with someone who is already in a relationship?
- To eat that ice cream, cake, or bag of chips when you are on a diet?
- To smoke when you have promised yourself that you will quit?
- To fudge the truth when you can get away with it?

Look carefully at yourself and make a list of what tempts you.

....

....

....

....

....

....

....

....

*T*emptation is a gift from the Universe that illuminates negativity in you so that you can recognize it before you act.

24
Temptation

A temptation is a dress rehearsal for a negative karmic event. Your temptations show you how powerful they are so that you can acknowledge, challenge, and change them.

A Temptation is a Dress Rehearsal

Make a list here of the things that tempt you or seem almost irresistible to you, such as:

- Drinking alcohol
- Eating food
- Having sex or looking at pornography
- Gambling
- Taking drugs
- Shopping

....

....

....

....

....

....

....

....

....

Now identify the one area that occupies most of your thoughts, images, and fantasies.

....

Consider these inner experiences as a private preview of what a frightened, out-of-control part of your personality is planning. Ask yourself, "Do I want to allow this part of my personality to remain out of control?"

Write what you discovered about yourself.

....

....

....

....

....

....

....

....

....

....

....

....

....

....

....

....

....

*T*emptation allows you to locate and heal parts of yourself within your own world of energy before your actions spill over into the worlds of others and create consequences you would not want to create.

*Temptation
shows you
what
you are
considering
so
you can
choose responsibly.*

*W*hen you use a temptation to excuse your decisions, you disempower yourself. You blame others, evil, or the Universe, and you do everything except look inside yourself, see how powerful the frightened parts of your personality are, and change them.

*Y*ou cannot gain strength from choices that do not stretch you.

The Power of Choice

The next time you are tempted . . .

- Stop.
- Take note of what sensations you feel in your solar plexus, chest, and throat areas when you don't act on your temptation.
- Consider the consequences of acting on your temptation.
- Ask yourself if you want to create those consequences.
- Remember that the power to indulge or challenge this frightened part of your personality is completely in your hands.
- Remind yourself, "This temptation is not stronger than who I want to become."
- Choose.

Repeat this each time you are tempted. Write here what you observe.

....

....

....

....

....

....

....

....

Temptation is not a power over you. You have the power.

The Gift of Temptation

When you are tempted, say these things to yourself:

- This is what I have I refused to acknowledge about myself in the past.
- This part of my personality is frightened and out of control.
- This is an opportunity for me to choose differently before I create painful consequences for myself.
- The power to say yes or no to this temptation is fully in my hands.

Write here what you learn as you use the gift of temptation wisely during the coming week.

....

....

....

....

....

....

....

....

....

....

25

Possible Futures

*E*very choice you make brings a possible future into your reality. When you choose without thinking about possible futures, the futures you choose are like your past, and your experiences become familiar and predictable.

It's Always My Choice

What behavior or reaction do you feel powerless to change in yourself, yet with which you would be willing to experiment choosing differently? For example, when you feel jealous, angry, or resentful, do the following:

- Remember what consequences this behavior or reaction has created for you in the past.
- Look for physical sensations in your throat, chest, and solar plexus areas and notice what thoughts you are having.

Write these observations here.

Follow these steps to a new choice:

- Decide what consequences you want to create in your future.
- Determine if now is the time to change this behavior or reaction.
- If yes, set your in-tention to make a different choice.
- Make a choice that will create consequences you are willing to accept responsibility for.
- If you find yourself reacting again, be gentle with yourself and start this process again.

Write what you discover in this Journal.

....

....

....

....

....

....

....

....

....

....

....

....

....

Your experiences
are not limited
to
what
you
have created
in the past.

My Past Is Not My Future
(Unless I Choose It)

Say these words to yourself with the energy of commitment:

- My experiences are not limited to what I have created in the past.
- At any moment, I can choose the possible future that I will bring into my reality.

Write your options here.

....

....

....

....

....

....

....

....

....

....

....

....

Decide how you will choose differently next time. Imagine yourself making this healthier choice, and write what you learn.

....

....

....

....

....

....

....

....

....

....

....

....

....

....

....

....

....

26

The Optimal Choice

*W*hen you make a choice, you walk through a doorway and it closes behind you, while other doorways that you could have chosen disappear, and new doorways appear before you. This is how you create the experiences of your life.

*E*ach time you make a choice, you bring a future into your reality, and as that future becomes your present, you must choose again.

Choose Again

Pick an example of something you do in your life repeatedly that has painful results and that you would like to change.

....

....

Every morning, say to yourself, "Each time I react in (anger, jealousy, and so on), I create a future that is different from the one I create if I respond with (for example, patience, kindness, and so on). What do I want to choose?"

How do you think your life would change if you responded rather than reacted?

....

....

....

....

....

....

....

*E*ach choice brings into your reality one of many possible futures.

Choice Maps

Can you remember a choice you made that brought you to your present situation? It might have been a choice to move to a new city, get married, change jobs, go to school, etc. Describe it here.

....

....

....

Now go back one layer and try to remember the prior choice that allowed you to make that choice. For example, the choice to move to a new city might have allowed you to meet the partner you chose to marry, or the choice to change jobs might have allowed you to accept an offer to move to another city. Describe the choice here.

....

....

....

Go back a few more layers, and try to remember the choices you made that lie beneath the choices you have already identified. Describe them here.

....

....

....

Now construct a diagram, or Choice Map, here. Start with a present circumstance, such as your location, job, or partner, and identify the choices that brought you to where you are now.

*T*he optimal choice is the choice your soul wants—to create harmony, cooperation, sharing, and reverence for Life.

Awareness Day

During the next twenty-four hours, try to remain aware of your choices, moment by moment.

Ask yourself these questions each time you make a choice:

- Am I willing to assume responsibility for the consequences this choice will create?
- Will this choice create harmony, cooperation, sharing, and reverence for Life?
- Is this the optimal choice I can make?

Write here what you learned.

....

....

....

....

....

....

....

....

....

Do this practice as often as necessary until your "awareness day" becomes a life of awareness.

The optimal choice is the choice to create authentic power. The creation of authentic power is a process, not an event. When you create authentic power, you use your life as it was meant to be used, and that is the optimal choice, whenever and however frequently you make it. Sooner or later you will begin to align your personality with your soul, but only you can decide when.

Part 5 Bonus Exercise

Bonus Exercise

During the next day, experiment with making the optimal choice for all choices you are aware of, and especially the choices that stretch you.

Write what you discover here.

....

....

....

....

....

....

....

....

....

....

....

We suggest that you continue this experiment for the next week. Consider our suggestion and decide if this option would be an optimal choice for you. Write here what you decide and why.

....

....

....

....

....

....

....

We suggest that you continue this experiment for the rest of your life. Consider our suggestion and decide if this option would be an optimal choice for you. Write here what you decide and why.

....

....

....

....

....

....

....

If you decide to make this experiment a part of your life, purchase a notebook that you feel good while holding, looking at, and writing in. Each day, write the optimal choices you made, and the choices you made that you do not feel were optimal. Continue writing in your journal as long as it is helpful to you, and refer back to this Journal whenever you feel it is appropriate.

A New Beginning

As you complete your first time through this Journal, apply what you have learned about responsible choice and about yourself. Appreciate what you have accomplished, and observe how far your in-tentions, commitment, and courage have brought you. Even if you choose to cease working with this Journal, your life will not be the same. You have begun the process of using your will to consciously create a life of joy, meaning, vitality, and fulfillment—not by avoiding that which is painful, but by experiencing it, learning from it, and changing it.

Go deep in your heart and see what you want to choose now. What in-tention do you want to set? For example, you may want to create harmony with individuals you feel separate from, use more of your creativity, appreciate yourself or others, share in deeper ways, listen instead of speak, or speak instead of listen. You may also want, to the best of your ability, to make all of your choices responsible choices. That is a very healthy in-tention. When your in-tention is clear to you, close this Journal and remain quietly with your in-tention. Whatever you choose, be gentle with yourself. That choice will create consequences you will enjoy.

Invitation to the Seat of the Soul Foundation

If you are interested in learning more about authentic power, please contact the Seat of the Soul Foundation, a 501(c)3 non-profit foundation cofounded by Gary Zukav and Linda Francis. There you can:

- Subscribe to the Foundation magazine, *Soul Source*.
- Enroll in Foundation events and apply for the three-year Creating Authentic Power Education program.
- Take authentic power courses online.
- Join an online community of spiritual partners.
- Join a Soul Circle.
- And more.

www.seatofthesoul.org

1-888-440-7685

1-541-482-8999 (from outside the United States)

welcome@seatofthesoul.org

You can also visit *www.zukav.com* and read the Soul Subject, Soul Question, and Soul Guest articles each month.

With love,

Gary and Linda

About the Authors

GARY ZUKAV is the author of *The Dancing Wu Li Masters: An Overview of the New Physics,* winner of The American Book Award for Science; *The Seat of the Soul,* the celebrated #1 bestseller in *The New York Times, USA Today, Los Angeles Times, Publishers Weekly,* and others; and *The New York Times* bestseller *Soul Stories.* His books have sold millions of copies and are published in twenty-four languages. He is a graduate of Harvard and a former U.S. Army Special Forces (Green Beret) officer with Vietnam service.

LINDA FRANCIS cocreated, with Gary Zukav, the *New York Times* bestseller *The Heart of the Soul: Emotional Awareness,* and is the cofounder, with Gary Zukav, of The Seat of the Soul Foundation, a nonprofit organization dedicated to assisting individuals in the creation of authentic power—the alignment of the personality with the soul. She has been in the healing profession for three decades, as a nurse and then as a chiropractor, and currently is cocreating curricula and co-leading events for The Seat of the Soul Foundation with Gary. They live in Oregon.